# MEAL IN A MUG

**80**
FAST, EASY
RECIPES
FOR
HUNGRY
PEOPLE

## ALL YOU NEED IS
## A MUG AND A MICROWAVE

# Denise Smart

**ATRIA** PAPERBACK
New York • London • Toronto • Sydney • New Delhi

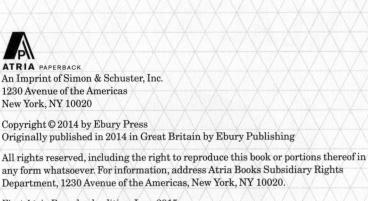

**ATRIA** PAPERBACK
An Imprint of Simon & Schuster, Inc.
1230 Avenue of the Americas
New York, NY 10020

First Atria Paperback edition June 2015

**ATRIA** PAPERBACK and colophon are trademarks of Simon & Schuster, Inc.

For information about special discounts for bulk purchases, please contact Simon & Schuster Special Sales at 1-866-506-1949 or business@simonandschuster.com.

The Simon & Schuster Speakers Bureau can bring authors to your live event. For more information or to book an event, contact the Simon & Schuster Speakers Bureau at 1-866-248-3049 or visit our website at www.simonspeakers.com.

Photography and props: Howard Shooter
Food stylist: Denise Smart

Manufactured in the United States of America

10  9  8  7  6  5  4  3  2  1

Library of Congress Cataloging-in-Publication Data

Smart, Denise.
   Meal in a mug : 80 fast, easy recipes for hungry people—all you need is a mug and a microwave / Denise Smart.
     pages cm
   Includes index.
   1. Quick and easy cooking.   2. Microwave cooking.   I. Title.
   TX833.5.S643   2015
   641.5'12—dc23                              2014050308

ISBN 978-1-4767-9814-1
ISBN 978-1-4767-9815-8 (ebook)

# CONTENTS

# INTRODUCTION

You like eating delicious food but don't have lots of fancy cooking equipment or much time to cook. Maybe you don't even have an oven. Or maybe you live on your own, or have just left home for the first time. Whether any of these scenarios describes you, or you're just looking for something different but easy for your mealtimes, then look no further: *Meal in a Mug* is the perfect book for you.

On the following pages, I'll prove to you that all you really need to make good food is a mug, a microwave, a handful of ingredients, and a few basic utensils. Here you'll find eighty recipes that cover every mealtime, from breakfast, lunch, and dinner to dessert, and those all-essential sweet or savory snacks. Some of the recipes don't even require any cooking!

So whether you're a student on a budget, stuck at the office and starving, or just can't be bothered to dirty a saucepan and preheat the oven, you're sure to find some ideas to satisfy every hungry moment and all your flavor cravings. This book will show you that in the time it would have taken to cook that packaged dinner or call your favorite restaurant for delivery, you could have created fresh, tasty food—from scratch.

## THINGS YOU NEED TO KNOW . . .

When preparing food for microwave cooking, remember these simple guidelines:

✳ **Important:** All recipes in this book were tested in a 1000-watt microwave.

✳ Microwave ovens vary, so you will need to adjust the cooking times accordingly. If unsure, check your machine's guidelines. A lower-wattage microwave will mean you'll need to cook food for slightly longer than the times given. In that case, it's best to add *just seconds,* as it's very easy to overcook.

✳ You can always cook food for a little longer, but you won't be able to "uncook" if you go too far. This is especially important for sweets and baking.

✳ Cut meat and vegetables into small, uniform sizes so that they cook evenly and quickly. Buy precut veggies when possible and save leftovers in the fridge.

✳ Mugs will be hot when removed from the oven, so use oven mitts or a kitchen towel and be careful when handling them.

✳ If food is covered during cooking, be sure to make a small hole in the top of the plastic wrap so steam doesn't build up and burn you when the covering is removed. Covering the food also helps to reduce splattering and helps it to cook more quickly.

✳ Most of the recipes say to allow for standing time once the food has been removed from the oven. This is so that the heat can continue to dissipate and finish cooking the food.

✳ Remember not to use any metal in the microwave, such as metal containers or foil.

✳ Stir the food as recommended to ensure even cooking.

✳ Some of the recipes state to stand the mug in a shallow microwaveable bowl; this is to catch any liquid that may boil over, which will save you from having to clean the microwave afterward.

✳ Remember, food cooked in a microwave will not brown, so some of the cakes may look less appealing than if they'd been baked in the oven. But the flavors will be just as good.

✳ Food heats more evenly at the edge of the microwave's carousel.

✳ I recommend boiling water in a kettle (stove or electric) since it's easy to overheat water in a microwave past the boiling point, and there's a chance it'll explode and burn you. But if you *do* boil water in the microwave, put a wooden chopstick or stir stick in the water to diffuse the heat and reduce the risk. Water doesn't bubble when heated to boiling in a microwave, so you can only know its temperature with a thermometer. In a 1000-watt oven, it takes approximately 1 minute on high to boil 1 cup of water.

## THINGS YOU'LL NEED ...

You don't need much, but you will need the following:

**Microwave:** Obviously.

**Selection of mugs:** Follow the size of the mugs used in the recipes; otherwise food may boil over, or it may over- or undercook. It's useful to have about three different sizes of microwaveable mugs: 17 fluid ounces (which I will refer to as large throughout); 10 fluid ounces (medium); and 5 to 7 fluid ounces (small). Tea and coffee cups can also be used, especially for some of the desserts.

**Measuring spoons:** A set of measuring spoons containing ½ teaspoon, 1 teaspoon, and 1 tablespoon is essential. Unless otherwise stated, all spoon measures in the recipes are level.

**Large measuring cup:** For measuring larger quantities of liquid.

**Fork and spoon:** Perfect for mixing and combining ingredients.

**Kitchen scissors:** For cutting up ingredients such as meat, herbs, and smaller vegetables.

**Kettle:** For boiling water to dissolve bouillon cubes and gelatin.

**Sharp knife:** A small knife is useful for cutting up larger pieces of meat and vegetables, or peeling vegetables if you don't have a peeler.

**Grater:** For grating cheese and removing the zest from citrus fruits.

## INGREDIENTS TO BUY SO YOU'LL NEVER BE HUNGRY ...

By keeping a selection of some of the following ingredients, you'll always be able to create a delicious meal. Any opened jars can be stored in the fridge. Buy small cans of tomatoes and beans so there will be less waste; any leftover canned food can be transferred to storage containers and kept in the fridge for a day or two.

## FOR YOUR PANTRY

Sunflower and olive oils
Canned chopped tomatoes
Canned beans, such as kidney beans, and chickpeas
Canned tuna or salmon
Canned corn
Canned pineapple
Tomato paste and ketchup
Soy sauce
Thai sweet chili sauce
Ginger and garlic pastes
Dried herbs and spices, such as chili powder, ground ginger, cumin, coriander, and dried mixed herbs
Curry pastes, such as Thai, Indian, and Moroccan
Packs of microwaveable rice

Long-grain and risotto rice
Noodles: egg and rice
Selection of pasta shapes
Couscous
Chocolate: dark, milk, and white
Canned evaporated milk
Sugar: superfine and light brown
Honey and molasses
Bouillon cubes and granules
Flour: all-purpose and self-rising
Baking powder
Baking soda

## FOR YOUR FRIDGE

Don't be tempted to buy too much fresh food; if you can, plan what you want to eat so that you don't end up with food spoiling. If you have to buy bigger quantities of fresh meat or fish, divide the remainder into usable amounts and store in freezer bags, labeled and dated.

Chicken breasts
Ground beef
Fresh chorizo
Bacon and ham
Salmon, cod, and shrimp
Milk
Butter
Cheese, such a Parmesan and Cheddar
Eggs
Heavy cream and crème fraîche
Fresh fruits and vegetables, such as peppers, onions, scallions, new potatoes, sweet potatoes, carrots, mushrooms, and tomatoes
Fresh pasta

## TO KEEP IN THE FREEZER

Even if you have only a small freezer, it is useful to have a few ingredients such as the following stored away. Remember to thaw meat and fish thoroughly before using.

Frozen shrimp
Frozen peas and spinach
Frozen berries, such as raspberries and mixed
Naan and pita bread
Ice cream


Got all that? Now you're ready to cook really fast, really tasty food.

# BREAKFAST

# EXTRA-CREAMY  OATMEAL

*Prep / cook time: 3 minutes*

*Microwave: 1000W
(see page 5)*

**5 tablespoons rolled oats**

**1 cup cold water**

**¼ cup evaporated milk**

**TO SERVE**

**Brown sugar, for sprinkling**

*This oatmeal is made really creamy by the addition of evaporated milk. You can substitute whole or reduced-fat milk, though, if you don't have any evaporated milk on hand.*

**1** Put the oats in a large mug or cup and add the water. Stir, then microwave on high for 1 minute.

**2** Remove from the microwave and stir in the evaporated milk. Return to the microwave and cook on high for 1 minute more. Stir well and allow to stand for 1 minute.

**3** Serve sprinkled with brown sugar to taste.

# PEANUT BUTTER AND JAM OATMEAL

SERVES 1

*Prep / cook time: 3 minutes*

*Microwave: 1000W*
*(see page 5)*

**5 tablespoons rolled oats**

**1 cup water**

**¼ cup milk**

**1 tablespoon chunky peanut butter**

**½ teaspoon sugar**

**TO SERVE**

**1 tablespoon strawberry jam**

*This might sound slightly unconventional, as you usually spread this combination on toast, but trust me: this oatmeal (pictured on page 8) tastes delicious!*

**1** Put the oats in a large mug or cup and add the water. Stir, then microwave on high for 1 minute.

**2** Remove from the microwave and stir in the milk. Return to the microwave and cook for 1 minute more. Stir in the peanut butter and sugar and allow the mixture to stand for 1 minute.

**3** Serve with a dollop of jam.

# SCRAMBLED EGGS

**SERVES 1**

*Prep / cook time: 2 minutes*

*Microwave: 1000W
(see page 5)*

**Pat of butter**

**2 eggs**

**1 tablespoon milk**

**Salt and freshly ground black pepper**

**TO SERVE**

**1 slice toast**

*The trick to microwaving eggs is to cook them slowly; overcooking will result in rubbery scrambled eggs— no one wants this. Other than that, feel free to ad lib; stir in any of your favorite fillings at the end.*

**1** Put the butter in a medium mug. Microwave on high for 20 to 30 seconds, until just melted.

**2** Break in the eggs, add the milk, and season with salt and pepper. Beat with a fork. Return to the microwave and cook on high for 30 seconds. Remove and break up the egg with the fork. Return to the microwave and cook on high for 10 seconds. Again, remove and break up with a fork. Repeat at 10-second intervals two more times.

**3** Remove from the microwave and beat again; the eggs will still look runny in places, but they will continue to cook. Allow to stand for 1 minute. Serve with toast.

***To make smoked salmon and chive scrambled eggs:***
Stir in 1 tablespoon chopped chives and a small handful of thinly sliced smoked salmon strips while the egg is still standing.

***To make goat cheese and tomato scrambled eggs:***
Stir in 2 tablespoons creamy goat cheese and 8 cherry tomato halves.

# EGGS FLORENTINE WITH HOLLANDAISE

**SERVES 1**

*Prep/cook time: 5 minutes*

*Microwave: 1000W (see page 5)*

2 generous tablespoons butter

1 egg yolk

2 teaspoons fresh lemon juice

Salt and freshly ground black pepper

Large handful of spinach

1 egg

**TO SERVE**

1 slice whole wheat toast

*This recipe makes more hollandaise than you'll need for one. Double the rest of the recipe and share with a friend, or cover the sauce and keep in the fridge for 2 to 3 days to serve cold.*

**1** Make the hollandaise sauce. Put the butter in a small mug and microwave on high for 10 seconds, until softened but not melted.

**2** Meanwhile, beat the egg yolk and lemon juice in a small cup and allow to stand for 1 minute.

**3** Add the yolk mixture to the softened butter. Microwave on high for 10 seconds, then beat well with a fork; the mixture may look lumpy but any lumps will disappear on whisking. Repeat twice, until the sauce is smooth and has thickened. Season with salt and pepper.

**4** Fill a large mug with the spinach (it will cook down). Cover with plastic wrap and pierce with a knife, then microwave on high for 2 minutes, until wilted.

**5** Meanwhile, bring water to a boil in a kettle and pour the water to come halfway up a small mug. Break in the egg, then microwave on low for 20 seconds. Repeat for 10 to 20 seconds more, until the egg is cooked to your liking.

**6** Place the spinach on the slice of toast, then top with the egg. Spoon over a little hollandaise sauce and serve.

# BREAKFAST MUFFIN

**SERVES 1**

*Prep / cook time: 5 minutes*

*Microwave: 1000W
(see page 5)*

**Butter, for greasing**

**¼ cup self-rising flour**

**½ teaspoon pumpkin pie spice**

**½ tablespoon pumpkin seeds**

**½ tablespoon sunflower seeds**

**2 tablespoons superfine sugar**

**2 tablespoons mashed banana**

**1 egg white, lightly beaten**

**2 tablespoons sunflower oil**

**2 tablespoons buttermilk or milk**

**12 fresh blueberries**

*This muffin is perfect for breakfast—it's packed with juicy blueberries, seeds, and banana. You can have it cold if you need to eat on the go, but it's especially delicious served warm.*

**1** Lightly butter a medium mug.

**2** Put the flour, pumpkin pie spice, pumpkin and sunflower seeds, and sugar in the mug and stir well.

**3** In a small bowl, beat the banana with the egg white, oil, and buttermilk, then stir into the dry ingredients in the mug, making sure you have mixed in all the flour from the bottom of the mug.

**4** Carefully stir in the blueberries. Stand the mug in a shallow microwaveable bowl as some of the blueberries may burst during heating and dribble down the sides.

**5** Microwave on high for 2 minutes 30 seconds, until risen and spongy, then allow to stand for 1 minute before serving.

# FULL ENGLISH BREAKFAST

**SERVES 1**

*Prep / cook time: 5 minutes*

*Microwave: 1000W*
*(see page 5)*

1 teaspoon sunflower oil

3 cocktail franks

3 mushrooms, quartered

1 slice Canadian bacon, chopped

¾ cup canned baked beans

**TO SERVE**

1 slice buttered toast

*Here's a complete breakfast in a mug. Although the franks won't brown in the microwave, once they're coated in the sauce used here, you'll never know.*

**1** Pour the oil into a large mug. Stir in the franks and mushrooms and microwave on high for 1 minute.

**2** Add the bacon and microwave on high for 1 minute. Stir in the beans. Cover with plastic wrap and pierce with a knife. Microwave on high for 1 minute, stir, then cover again and cook for 1 minute more.

**3** Allow to stand for 1 minute before serving with a slice of buttered toast.

# BACON AND TOMATO MUFFIN

**SERVES 1**

*Prep / cook time: 7 minutes*

*Microwave: 1000W
(see page 5)*

1 tablespoon butter, melted, plus extra for greasing

1 slice Canadian bacon, chopped

¼ cup self-rising flour

3 tablespoons finely grated Cheddar cheese

3 sun-dried tomatoes, chopped

1 tablespoon chopped chives

¼ cup plus 3 tablespoons (7 tablespoons) buttermilk or milk

1 egg, beaten

Pinch of salt and freshly ground black pepper

*This savory muffin is delicious served warm and makes a satisfying breakfast or brunch. Pair it up with a Vanilla Latte (see page 124) for your first meal of the day.*

**1** Lightly butter a large mug. Put in the bacon and microwave on high for 1 minute. Stir to break up the bacon.

**2** Add the flour, 2 tablespoons of the Cheddar, the sun-dried tomatoes, and chives and stir well. Add the buttermilk, melted butter, egg, salt, and pepper and mix well with a fork until all the ingredients are combined. Sprinkle the top with the remaining Cheddar.

**3** Microwave on high for 4 minutes, then allow to stand for 1 minute. Turn out of the mug and allow to cool slightly before eating.

# SMOKED HADDOCK KEDGEREE

**SERVES 1**

*Prep / cook time: 4 minutes*

*Microwave: 1000W (see page 5)*

**2 teaspoons mild curry paste**

**3 tablespoons water**

**¾ cup cooked microwaveable pilaf rice**

**1 teaspoon butter, softened**

**¼ cup small chunks smoked haddock (about 2 ounces)**

**1 tablespoon chopped fresh parsley**

**2 teaspoons fresh lemon juice**

**1 egg**

**Freshly ground black pepper**

*Kedgeree is a traditional British breakfast with Indian origins made with cooked flaked fish and rice. You can also enjoy it for lunch or dinner!*

**1** Mix the curry paste with 1 tablespoon of the water in a medium mug. Add the rice and butter and stir well.

**2** Gently stir in the fish and the remaining 2 tablespoons water. Cover with plastic wrap and pierce with a knife. Microwave on high for 1 minute.

**3** Remove from the microwave and stir in the parsley and lemon juice. Make a well in the center of the rice and break in the egg. Cover again with plastic wrap and microwave on high for 1 minute to 1 minute 30 seconds, until the egg is just cooked.

**4** Allow to stand for 1 minute, then serve with pepper to taste.

# BIRCHER MUESLI

**SERVES 1**

Prep time: 5 minutes,
plus soaking time

¼ **cup rolled oats**

**1 small apple, grated**

¾ **cup milk**

**1 tablespoon chopped almonds**

**2 tablespoons fresh raspberries**

**2 tablespoons fresh blueberries**

### TO SERVE

**Scattering of pumpkin and
sunflower seeds**

**Honey or maple syrup**

*Mix up the ingredients the night before and you'll
have a delicious breakfast ready the next morning.
Try adding a selection of dried fruits instead of
fresh for a texture treat.*

**1** Mix the oats, apple, milk, almonds, raspberries, and
blueberries in a medium mug or cup. Cover and place in
the fridge for 1 to 2 hours or overnight, so that the oats
absorb the liquid.

**2** Stir before serving and add a little extra milk if you
prefer a runnier consistency. Sprinkle with the pumpkin
and sunflower seeds, drizzle with some honey, and grab
your spoon!

# GRANOLA

SERVES 2

*Prep / cook time: 3 minutes*

*Microwave: 1000W*
*(see page 5)*

2 tablespoons honey

1 tablespoon oil

Pinch of salt

1 teaspoon ground cinnamon

¾ cup rolled oats

12 almonds

1 tablespoon pumpkin seeds

½ tablespoon sunflower seeds

2 tablespoons raisins

**TO SERVE**

Fresh fruit

Yogurt

Honey

*This is so simple to make. Add your favorite dried fruits, such as cranberries, blueberries, or chopped apricots. This recipe serves two, but any leftover granola can be stored in an airtight container for up to one week.*

**1** Place 1 tablespoon of the honey, the oil, salt, and cinnamon into a large mug. Microwave on high for 30 seconds.

**2** Add the oats and stir to coat them with the honey mixture. Microwave on high for 1 minute, then stir in the almonds and pumpkin and sunflower seeds.

**3** Microwave on high for 1 minute and stir again. Stir in the remaining 1 tablespoon honey and the raisins and allow to cool.

**4** Serve with fresh fruit, yogurt, and a drizzle of honey for a real early morning treat.

# HUEVO RANCHERO

SERVES
1

*Cook / prep time: 3 minutes*

*Microwave: 1000W
(see page 5)*

**1 corn tortilla**

**3 tablespoons tomato salsa**

**1 egg**

**1 tablespoon chopped fresh cilantro**

*Huevos rancheros, or "ranch-style eggs," are breakfast favorites, and they're really easy to make. With a spice hit of salsa, this egg recipe is quick to cook and uses just a few simple ingredients.*

**1** Cut the tortilla into 4 wedges and place them in the base and sides of a medium microwaveable coffee cup.

**2** Spoon in the salsa. Cover with plastic wrap and pierce with a knife, then microwave on high for 1 minute.

**3** Remove from the microwave and make a well in the salsa. Crack in the egg.

**4** Cover again with the plastic wrap, then return to the microwave and cook on low for 1 minute for a soft yolk. (If you prefer a harder yolk, cook for 30 seconds more.) Allow to stand for 1 minute before sprinkling with the cilantro and serving.

# LUNCH

# SHRIMP LAKSA

**SERVES 1**

Prep / cook time: 5 minutes

Microwave: 1000W
(see page 5)

**Large handful (2 ounces) flat dried rice noodles**

**¼ cup plus 3 tablespoons (7 tablespoons) fish stock**

**1 tablespoon laksa paste**

**3 tablespoons coconut cream**

**½ teaspoon fish sauce**

**6 cooked shelled jumbo shrimp**

**Small handful bean sprouts**

**8 slices canned bamboo shoots, drained**

**1 tablespoon chopped fresh cilantro**

**TO SERVE**

**1 scallion, chopped**

**½ small fresh red chile, finely sliced**

*Laksa is a spicy, fragrant coconut noodle soup (pictured on page 26). If shrimp isn't your thing, replace them with a handful of cooked shredded chicken and change the fish stock to chicken stock.*

**1** Break the noodles in half and put them in a large mug. Add the stock and stir, then microwave on high for 1 minute. Stir well.

**2** Stir in the laksa paste, coconut cream, and fish sauce and microwave on high for 1 minute.

**3** Stir in the shrimp, bean sprouts, and bamboo shoots and microwave on high for 1 minute, or until the shrimp are heated through. Stir in the cilantro.

**4** To serve, top with the scallion and chile.

# PEA AND PESTO SOUP

**SERVES 1**

*Prep / cook time: 6 minutes*

*Microwave: 1000W*
*(see page 5)*

**2 medium red potatoes, peeled and chopped into ¾-inch chunks**

**1 scallion, chopped**

**1 cup hot vegetable stock**

**½ cup frozen peas**

**1 teaspoon pesto**

**TO SERVE**

**Baguette slices**

*You can use pesto from a jar or chilled fresh pesto to make this simple soup. For a bit more texture, try scattering a little crumbled feta on top.*

**1** Put the potatoes and scallion in a large mug. Add 3 tablespoons of the stock. Cover with plastic wrap and pierce with a knife. Microwave on high for 2 minutes, until tender. Stir in the peas, cover, and microwave on high for 1 minute.

**2** Stand the mug in a shallow microwaveable dish, in case any liquid boils over. Stir in the remaining stock, cover again with the plastic wrap, and microwave on high for 2 minutes, or until the peas are tender.

**3** Mash the peas and potatoes with a fork until coarsely crushed, or use a stick blender if you have one. Stir in the pesto.

**4** Serve with baguette slices.

# SMOKED HADDOCK CHOWDER

**SERVES 1**

*Prep / cook time: 5 minutes*

*Microwave: 1000W
(see page 5)*

**1 teaspoon sunflower oil**

**1 tablespoon chopped onion**

**1 slice bacon, chopped**

**1 small potato, peeled and cut into ½-inch cubes**

**¼ cup plus 3 tablespoons (7 tablespoons) water**

**¼ cup plus 3 tablespoons (7 tablespoons) milk**

**¼ cup canned corn, drained**

**¼ cup skinless smoked haddock pieces**

**Handful of baby spinach leaves**

**Freshly ground black pepper**

**TO SERVE**

**Crusty bread**

*Satisfying and warming, this chowder is a creamy soup that combines smoky bacon and smoked haddock for a rich, hearty flavor.*

**1** Pour the oil into a large mug. Add the onion and bacon and microwave on high for 30 seconds.

**2** Add the potato and water and microwave on high for 2 minutes. Add the milk, corn, and haddock and microwave for 1 minute. Stir gently and microwave on high for 30 seconds to 1 minute more, or until the fish starts to flake and the potatoes are tender.

**3** Stir in the spinach, and allow to stand for 1 minute. Season to taste with pepper.

**4** Serve with crusty bread.

# CHORIZO AND LIMA BEAN SALAD

**SERVES 1**

Prep / cook time: 3 minutes

Microwave: 1000W
(see page 5)

---

1 small fresh chorizo sausage
(about 1.5 ounces), sliced crosswise

¾ cup canned lima beans,
drained and rinsed

6 cherry tomatoes, halved

1 teaspoon sherry vinegar

2 teaspoons chopped fresh parsley

Freshly ground black pepper

**TO SERVE**

Crusty bread

*This is so quick to prepare, and the paprika oil from the chorizo and the sherry vinegar make a perfect "instant dressing."*

**1** Put the chorizo in a large mug and microwave on high for 1 minute, until the oil is released.

**2** Stir in the lima beans, tomatoes, and vinegar, return to the microwave, and cook on high for 30 seconds. Stir again and add the parsley.

**3** Season to taste with pepper and serve with a chunk of crusty bread.

# GOAT CHEESE, BASIL, AND TOMATO QUICHE

**SERVES 1**

*Prep / cook time: 3 minutes*

*Microwave: 1000W (see page 5)*

2 eggs

2 tablespoons milk

Salt and freshly ground black pepper

4 basil leaves, roughly torn

4 sun-dried or cherry tomatoes, halved

2 tablespoons chopped goat cheese

1 tablespoon freshly grated Parmesan cheese

**TO SERVE**

Handful of baby arugula

*This is a healthier option than a traditional quiche made with a pastry base, but it's just as tasty. Serve it with an arugula salad for a quick, satisfying lunch.*

**1** Break the eggs into a medium microwaveable coffee cup. Add the milk, salt, and pepper and beat thoroughly, then stir in the basil, tomatoes, and goat cheese. Sprinkle the Parmesan over the top.

**2** Microwave on high for 2 minutes. Remove and allow to stand for 1 minute before serving with a handful of arugula.

# PESTO ORZO SALAD

**SERVES 1**

*Prep / cook time: 8 minutes*

*Microwave: 1000W*
*(see page 5)*

**¼ cup orzo pasta**

**⅔ cup boiling water**

**2 tablespoons pesto**

**4 cherry tomatoes, halved or quartered**

**4 mini mozzarella balls or pearls, torn in half**

**1 tablespoon toasted pine nuts**

**Handful of baby arugula**

*Orzo is a tiny pasta that looks like rice. In this simple salad it is combined with the Italian flavors of tomatoes, mozzarella, and basil.*

**1** Put the orzo in a large mug. Add ¼ cup of the boiling water and microwave on high for 2 minutes. Stir well to break up the pasta, than add another ¼ cup of boiling water and microwave on high for 2 minutes.

**2** Remove from the microwave and stir in the remaining boiling water. Return to the microwave and cook on high for 1 minute. Stir well and allow to stand for 2 minutes, then stir in the pesto.

**3** Add the tomatoes, mozzarella, and pine nuts and stir in the arugula. Serve immediately.

# COUSCOUS WITH MINT, FETA, AND POMEGRANATE

**SERVES 1**

*Prep / cook time: 5 minutes*

¼ **cup couscous**

**Grated zest and juice of ½ lemon**

**4 Peppadew peppers, from a jar, halved**

**3 tablespoons crumbled feta cheese**

**3 tablespoons pomegranate seeds**

**1 tablespoon chopped fresh mint**

**1 teaspoon olive oil**

**Salt and freshly ground black pepper**

**TO SERVE**

**Pita bread**

*This refreshing salad is perfect for a light lunch. Serve with pita bread.*

**1** Put the couscous in a large mug and add enough boiling water to cover. Cover with plastic wrap and allow to stand for 3 to 4 minutes, or until the water has been absorbed.

**2** Fluff the couscous with a fork, then stir in the lemon zest and juice and allow to cool. Stir in the Peppadews, feta, pomegranate seeds, mint, and oil. Season to taste with salt and pepper and stir well.

**3** Serve immediately with pita bread.

# REFRIED BEAN WRAP

**SERVES 1**

*Prep / cook time: 3 minutes*

*Microwave: 1000W*
*(see page 5)*

**3 tablespoons canned refried beans**

**1 large flour tortilla**

**1 scallion, chopped**

**3 pickled jalapeño pepper slices (optional)**

**1 tablespoon chopped fresh cilantro**

**2 tablespoons tomato salsa**

**¼ cup grated Cheddar cheese**

*Vary the ingredients here to suit your tastes—try it with cooked shredded chicken, for instance, but remember to keep the cheese and salsa so that it holds together. Top it with some sour cream and guacamole for a more substantial meal. This is best eaten with a fork, accompanied by some crisp lettuce leaves.*

**1** Spread the beans over the tortilla, leaving a ¾-inch border. Sprinkle it with the scallion, jalapeños (if using), and cilantro. Top with the salsa and sprinkle with the cheese.

**2** Fold over the sides of the tortilla, then roll it up from the bottom to securely encase the ingredients.

**3** Place in a tall, narrow mug and microwave on high for 1 minute 30 seconds (don't worry if the tortilla collapses slightly). Allow to stand for 1 minute before serving.

# THAI BEEF NOODLE SALAD

**SERVES 1**

*Prep / cook time: 5 minutes*

1 nest instant rice
vermicelli noodles

Small chunk of cucumber

Juice of 1 small lime

2 tablespoons Thai sweet chili
sauce

2 teaspoons reduced sodium soy
sauce

1 small carrot, peeled and
cut into thin strips

1 scallion, finely chopped

1 or 2 slices cooked roast beef,
cut into thin strips

Small handful of chopped
fresh cilantro

1 tablespoon dry-roasted peanuts,
chopped (optional)

*If time permits, allow this salad to stand for 10 to
15 minutes in order to allow the flavors to develop.
Otherwise, you can simply prepare it in advance, then
cover and refrigerate it until ready to eat.*

**1** Put the noodles in a large mug (you may have to break
the nest in half). Cover with boiling water and allow to
stand for 3 minutes. Drain in a sieve and rinse under
cold running water, then drain well.

**2** Meanwhile, halve the cucumber lengthwise, then scoop
out the seeds with a teaspoon and discard them. Slice
the flesh thinly.

**3** Mix the lime juice, chili sauce, and soy sauce in the
mug. Add the noodles and stir to coat well. Add the
cucumber, carrot, scallion, beef, and cilantro. Toss
together using 2 forks until all the ingredients are coated
with the dressing.

**4** Sprinkle with the peanuts (if using) and serve.

# MISO CHICKEN NOODLE SOUP

**SERVES 1**

*Prep / cook time: 5 minutes*

*Microwave: 1000W
(see page 5)*

**1 teaspoon miso paste**

**½ teaspoon ginger paste
or chopped ginger**

**1¼ cups hot chicken stock**

**1 nest fine egg noodles**

**Small handful of shredded
cooked roast chicken**

**1 scallion, chopped**

**2 tablespoons fresh or frozen
edamame**

*This healthy Japanese-inspired soup is
aromatic and filling—just perfect for a speedy,
nutritious lunch.*

**1** Put the miso paste and ginger paste in a large mug.
Pour in the stock and stir well.

**2** Add the noodles and place the mug in a shallow
microwaveable bowl, in case any of the liquid should boil
over. Microwave on high for 2 minutes.

**3** Remove from the microwave, stir well, then add the
chicken, scallion, and edamame. Microwave on high for
1 minute, or until the chicken and edamame are heated
through.

**4** Allow to stand for 1 minute, then serve.

# SPICY LENTIL AND BACON SOUP

**SERVES 1**

*Prep / cook time: 10 minutes*

*Microwave: 1000W
(see page 5)*

1 teaspoon sunflower oil

1 slice bacon, chopped

2 tablespoons chopped onion

½ teaspoon ground cumin

¼ teaspoon ground turmeric

1 small carrot, peeled and diced

¼ cup red lentils

1¼ cups hot chicken
or vegetable stock

Pinch of red pepper flakes

**TO SERVE**

Naan bread

*Dried red lentils are a perfect ingredient to keep in your pantry. Great for hearty soups, they can also be used to make tasty curried dishes such as dals.*

**1** Put the oil, bacon, onion, cumin, and turmeric in a large mug and stir well. Microwave on high for 1 minute. Stir in the carrot and lentils.

**2** Add ½ cup of the stock and stand the mug in a shallow microwaveable bowl. Microwave on high for 2 minutes. Stir and microwave on high for 2 minutes more.

**3** Stir in another ½ cup of the stock and add the red pepper flakes. Microwave on high for 2 minutes.

**4** Stir in the remaining stock and microwave on high for 1 minute, until the lentils are tender. Allow to stand for 1 minute and serve with naan bread.

# SNACKS AND SIDES

**SERVES 1**

# POPCORN

*Prep / cook time: 2 minutes*

*Microwave: 1000W
(see page 5)*

**2 teaspoons sunflower oil**

**2 tablespoons popcorn**

**Salt or sugar, for sprinkling
(optional)**

*The hardest part of making your own popcorn
(pictured on page 44) is choosing the flavor. Once
you've decided, take 2 minutes to make a batch before
you settle down to watch that movie . . .*

**1** Pour the oil into a large mug and add the popcorn.
Cover with plastic wrap and pierce with a knife.

**2** Microwave on high for 1 minute. Using a kitchen towel
or oven mitts (the mug will get hot!), remove from the
microwave and shake the mug.

**3** Return to the microwave and cook on high for 1 minute
more. Remove from the microwave and allow to stand
for 1 minute.

**4** Sprinkle with a little salt or sugar (if using) and enjoy!

***To make spiced smoked paprika popcorn:***
Prepare the popcorn as in the basic recipe above. While the
popcorn is standing, mix 1 teaspoon smoked paprika, ½ teaspoon
ground cumin, ½ teaspoon ground black pepper, and a pinch of
salt in a small cup. Sprinkle the spices over the warm popcorn
and drizzle with 1 teaspoon olive oil. Cover the mug again and
shake it well so all the popcorn is well coated. Serve immediately.

***To make cocoa and marshmallow popcorn:***
Prepare the popcorn as in the basic recipe above, but use
1 teaspoon oil and 1 tablespoon popcorn. Allow to stand for
1 minute, then add 1 tablespoon hot cocoa mix and 2 tablespoons
mini marshmallows and stir well.

# LEMON AND CHILE WEDGES

SERVES 1

*Prep / cook time: 5 minutes*

*Microwave: 1000W (see page 5)*

1 medium sweet potato, scrubbed and cut into small wedges

3 wedges lemon

1 small red chile pepper, seeded and finely chopped (optional)

1 tablespoon chopped fresh cilantro

Salt and freshly ground black pepper

½ teaspoon olive oil

*These wedges won't crisp up like oven-baked ones, but they're still delicious. If you prefer, roughly crush the potatoes with the back of a fork.*

**1** Stand the potato wedges in a tall large mug. Add the lemon wedges.

**2** Cover with plastic wrap and pierce with a knife. Microwave on high for 4 minutes. Allow to stand for 1 minute, then carefully remove the lemon wedges with a fork and squeeze the juice over the potatoes. Scatter on the chile (if using), then the cilantro. Season to taste with salt and black pepper and drizzle with the oil before serving.

# CHEESY NACHOS

**SERVES 1**

*Cooking time: 1 minute*

*Microwave: 1000W*
*(see page 5)*

**12 tortilla chips**

**2 tablespoons tomato salsa**

**2 tablespoons grated Cheddar cheese**

**6 pickled jalapeño pepper slices**

**TO SERVE**

**Sour cream and/or guacamole**

*Cheaper than the restaurant equivalent, and so quick to prepare, this is another great sofa snack.*

**1** Layer about 6 tortilla chips in the base and sides of a medium microwaveable coffee cup.

**2** Spoon over 1 tablespoon of the salsa, 1 tablespoon of the Cheddar, and a few jalapeño slices. Repeat the layers, finishing with the Cheddar.

**3** Microwave on high for 1 minute.

**4** Serve topped with a little sour cream or guacamole (or both!).

# EGG FRIED RICE

SERVES 1

*Prep / cook time: 5 minutes*

*Microwave: 1000W (see page 5)*

¾ cup cooked long-grain microwave rice

2 tablespoons frozen peas

1 small slice ham, diced

1 scallion, chopped

Small handful of bean sprouts

1 egg

1 teaspoon reduced sodium soy sauce

½ teaspoon sesame oil

*This rice makes a perfect accompaniment to any Chinese dish. Alternatively, why not make it into a main meal by adding some cooked peeled shrimp?*

**1** Put the rice in a medium mug. Cover with plastic wrap and pierce with a knife. Microwave on high for 1 minute.

**2** Stir in the peas, ham, scallion, and bean sprouts, cover again, and microwave on high for 1 minute.

**3** In a small bowl, beat the egg with the soy sauce and oil. Add this mixture to the mug and stir into the rice. Cover again with the plastic wrap and microwave on high for 30 seconds. Stir, then allow to stand for 1 minute before serving.

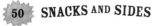

# GARLICKY MUSHROOMS

**SERVES 1**

Prep / cook time: 3 minutes

Microwave: 1000W
(see page 5)

**20 button mushrooms**

**1 garlic clove (crushed in a garlic press or smashed with a knife)**

**1 teaspoon butter, softened**

**1 tablespoon chopped fresh parsley**

**Salt and freshly ground black pepper**

**TO SERVE**

**Bread or toasted brioche**

*This is an indulgent snack, especially when served on a slice of toasted brioche.*

**1** Put the mushrooms, garlic, and butter in a medium mug. Cover with plastic wrap and pierce with a knife. Microwave on high for 1 minute.

**2** Stir well, then return to the microwave and cook on high for 30 seconds. Stir in the parsley and season to taste with salt and pepper.

**3** Serve with some bread to mop up the garlic butter.

# CAULIFLOWER CHEESE

**SERVES 1**

*Prep / cook time: 6 minutes, plus 3 to 4 minutes standing time*

*Microwave: 1000W (see page 5)*

1 tablespoon butter

1 tablespoon all-purpose flour

⅔ cup milk

½ teaspoon Dijon mustard

3 tablespoons finely grated Gruyère cheese

8 small cauliflower florets

Salt and freshly ground black pepper

*This cheesy cauliflower is made using Gruyère, which adds a nutty flavor, but you can always use a mature Cheddar if you like. Serve as a meal on its own or as an easy side dish.*

**1** Put the butter, flour, and milk in a large mug. Microwave on high for 30 seconds, then whisk. Return to the microwave and cook for another 30 seconds, then whisk again. Repeat until the sauce thickens. Don't be tempted to ignore the 30-second intervals or the sauce may go lumpy!

**2** Stir in the mustard and Gruyère and stir until the Gruyère melts. Add the cauliflower and stir to coat with the cheese sauce. Cover the mug with plastic wrap and pierce with a knife, return it to the microwave, and cook on medium for 3 to 4 minutes, or until the cauliflower is tender. Season to taste with salt and pepper.

**3** Allow to stand for 3 to 4 minutes before serving, as the sauce will be very hot.

# ROSEMARY GARLIC POTATOES

**SERVES 1**

*Prep / cook time: 4 minutes*

*Microwave: 1000W
(see page 5)*

**2 teaspoons butter, softened**

**1 garlic clove (crushed in a garlic press or smashed with a knife)**

**5 baby red potatoes**

**1 teaspoon chopped fresh rosemary**

**Salt and freshly ground black pepper**

*These delicious potatoes are so quick to cook, you'll hardly believe you've made them yourself. You could substitute some chopped fresh thyme for the rosemary to change the flavor.*

**1** Put the butter and garlic in a medium cup or mug. Microwave on high for 30 seconds.

**2** Stir in the potatoes and rosemary and season well with salt and pepper, then stir to coat the potatoes with the garlic butter. Cover with plastic wrap and pierce with a knife.

**3** Microwave on high for 2 to 3 minutes, or until the potatoes are tender. Allow to stand for 1 minute before serving.

# HONEYED CARROTS

SERVES
1

*Prep / cook time: 3 minutes*

*Microwave: 1000W
(see page 5)*

**7 baby carrots**

**1 teaspoon butter**

**1 teaspoon honey**

**Salt and freshly ground
black pepper**

*Give your carrots a slightly sweet taste with the
addition of honey for this simple but elegant side dish.*

**1** Put the carrots, butter, honey, and salt and pepper to
taste in a large mug. Microwave on high for 2 minutes.

**2** Stir well, then microwave on high for 1 minute more,
or until the carrots are just tender.

**3** Allow to stand for 1 minute before serving.

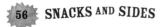

# POTATO DAUPHINOISE

**SERVES 1**

*Prep / cook time: 6 minutes*

*Microwave: 1000W
(see page 5)*

Butter, for greasing

¼ cup plus 3 tablespoons
(7 tablespoons) heavy cream

1 tablespoon milk

1 garlic clove (crushed in a
garlic press or smashed with
a knife)

1 teaspoon chopped fresh
rosemary

Salt and freshly ground
black pepper

2 small potatoes, peeled
and very thinly sliced

*This rich and indulgent French potato recipe makes
a wonderful side dish, but it's delicious enough to eat
as a meal on its own.*

**1** Lightly butter a medium mug.

**2** In a small measuring cup, stir the cream, milk, garlic,
and rosemary. Season well with salt and pepper.

**3** Place a couple of layers of potatoes in the mug and pour
in a little of the cream mixture. Continue layering and
pouring over a little more of the cream until the potatoes
are about 1 inch from the top of the mug. Finish with any
remaining cream mixture.

**4** Cover the mug with plastic wrap and pierce with a
knife. Stand the mug in a microwaveable shallow bowl,
in case any of the mixture boils over. Microwave on
medium for 4 to 5 minutes, or until a knife goes easily
through the potatoes.

**5** Allow to stand for 1 minute before serving.

 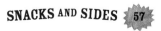

SERVES
2

# CORNBREAD

*Prep / cook time: 4 minutes*

*Microwave: 1000W
(see page 5)*

2 tablespoons all-purpose flour

2 tablespoons coarse cornmeal or
polenta

½ teaspoon baking powder

Pinch of salt and freshly
ground black pepper

1 scallion, chopped

1 red chile pepper, seeded
and chopped (optional)

2 tablespoons canned corn,
drained

½ cup buttermilk or milk

1 tablespoon butter, melted

1 egg

*Cornbread is soft and moist, so allow it to cool slightly
before slicing it into rounds. It makes a perfect
accompaniment to Chili con Carne (see page 76) or
with soup (see pages 28 to 30). For cornbread with a
kick, add a chopped red chile.*

**1** In a large mug, mix the flour, cornmeal, baking powder,
salt, black pepper, scallion, chile (if using), and corn.

**2** In a bowl, whisk the buttermilk, melted butter, and egg
and stir into the dry ingredients in the mug. Mix well
until all the ingredients are combined.

**3** Microwave on high for 2 minutes. Allow to stand for
1 minute, then turn out and serve.

# FRUITY COUSCOUS

**SERVES 1**

*Prep/cook time: 5 minutes*

*Microwave: 1000W*
*(see page 5)*

¼ **cup couscous**

**Finely grated zest and juice of ½ lemon**

**2 tablespoons toasted pine nuts**

**2 tablespoons raisins**

**1 scallion, finely chopped**

**1 tablespoon chopped fresh parsley**

*This couscous makes a perfect partner for the Sweet Potato and Chickpea Tagine (see page 84), but it also makes a satisfying sweet-savory snack on its own.*

**1** Put the couscous in a medium mug and pour in enough boiling water to cover. Cover the mug with plastic wrap and allow to stand for 3 to 4 minutes, or until the water has been absorbed.

**2** Fluff the couscous with a fork, then stir in the lemon zest and juice, pine nuts, raisins, scallion, and parsley. Serve immediately.

# CHOCOLATE PEANUT BUTTER COOKIE

**SERVES 1**

*Prep / cook time: 3 minutes*

*Microwave: 1000W (see page 5)*

**1 tablespoon butter, softened**

**2 teaspoons chunky peanut butter**

**2 tablespoons light brown sugar**

**Pinch of salt**

**¼ teaspoon vanilla extract**

**1 egg yolk**

**1 teaspoon milk**

**3 tablespoons all-purpose flour**

**2 tablespoons dark or milk chocolate chips**

*Craving a cookie but don't fancy baking a whole batch? Just follow this recipe for a quick fix. Serve it warm with a scoop of chocolate or vanilla ice cream.*

**1** Put the butter and peanut butter in a medium mug or microwaveable teacup. Microwave on high for 30 seconds, then remove and stir the mixture until completely melted.

**2** Stir in the brown sugar, salt, vanilla, egg yolk, and milk. Add the flour and stir until the mixture is well combined.

**3** Add the chocolate chips and mix until the chips are evenly distributed. Flatten the top with the back of a spoon.

**4** Microwave on high for 40 to 50 seconds, or until the dough is just cooked. Allow to stand for 1 minute so that the cookie finishes cooking.

# CHEESE AND CHIVE SCONES

**SERVES 2**

*Prep / cook time: 4 minutes*

*Microwave: 1000W*
*(see page 5)*

¼ **cup all-purpose flour**

½ **teaspoon baking powder**

¼ **teaspoon mustard powder**

¼ **teaspoon salt**

**Pinch of cayenne pepper**

**Freshly ground black pepper**

**2 tablespoons butter, cut into small pieces**

**3 tablespoons finely grated sharp Cheddar cheese**

**1 tablespoon chopped chives**

½ **beaten egg**

**2 tablespoons milk**

*This would be the perfect partner for a bowl of steaming soup. Use a chopped scallion instead of the chives if that's all you have in the fridge. Spread the scone with a little butter and eat it while it's still warm.*

**1** Put the flour in a wide medium mug or cup (this makes it easier to rub in the butter—see below). Stir in the baking powder, mustard, salt, cayenne, and black pepper to taste.

**2** Using your fingertips, rub in the butter until the mixture resembles fine bread crumbs. Stir in most of the Cheddar (reserving a little for the top) and the chives.

**3** Add the egg and milk and mix with a fork until all the ingredients are incorporated and you have a sticky dough. Sprinkle with the reserved Cheddar and cook on high for 1 minute 30 seconds. Allow to stand for 1 minute.

**4** Turn out of the cup and cut into slices.

# CHOC-CHIP MUFFINS

**SERVES 2**

*Prep / cook time: 5 minutes*

*Microwave: 1000W*
*(see page 5)*

¼ cup self-rising flour

¼ cup light brown sugar

1 tablespoon unsweetened cocoa powder

2 tablespoons lightly whisked egg white

½ teaspoon vanilla extract

3 tablespoons milk

3 tablespoons sunflower oil

3 tablespoons dark chocolate chips

*These chocolatey muffins are best served warm. To make things even easier, you could also mix all the ingredients together in a medium cup to create one large muffin.*

**1** Put a paper muffin liner in the base of each of 2 small coffee cups (or line them with parchment paper).

**2** In a small bowl, mix the flour, brown sugar, cocoa powder, egg white, vanilla, and 1 tablespoon of the milk to make a smooth paste.

**3** Stir in the remaining 2 tablespoons milk, the oil, and 2 tablespoons of the chocolate chips.

**4** Divide the chocolate mixture between the 2 cups, then sprinkle the top with the remaining 1 tablespoon chocolate chips.

**5** Microwave on high for 3 minutes. Allow to stand for 1 minute before serving.

# MAINS

# CHICKEN KORMA

SERVES
1

Prep / cook time: 8 minutes

Microwave: 1000W
(see page 5)

1 small boneless, skinless chicken breast, cut into small pieces

½ teaspoon garlic paste

½ teaspoon ginger paste

½ teaspoon hot chili powder

½ teaspoon tomato paste

½ teaspoon ground coriander

¼ teaspoon ground turmeric

2 tablespoons ground almonds

2 cardamom pods, lightly crushed

¼ cup plain whole-milk yogurt

1 tablespoon half-and-half

½ teaspoon garam masala

2 tablespoons sliced almonds

## TO SERVE

Naan bread or rice

*For stronger flavors, marinate the chicken for 2 to 3 hours or overnight in the fridge if you wish. Serve it with a warm ready-made naan bread, or stir in some cooked rice and microwave on high for 1 minute. (Pictured on page 64.)*

**1** In a large mug, combine the chicken, garlic paste, ginger paste, chili powder, tomato paste, coriander, turmeric, and ground almonds. Mix well. Stand the mug in a shallow microwaveable bowl, in case any mixture overflows.

**2** Cover with plastic wrap and pierce with a knife. Microwave on high for 2 minutes. Stir well, then return to the microwave and cook on low for 4 minutes.

**3** Stir in the half-and-half, garam masala, and sliced almonds and allow to stand for 1 minute before serving with naan bread or rice.

# THAI SHRIMP CURRY

*Prep / cook time: 8 minutes*

*Microwave: 1000W
(see page 5)*

1 tablespoon Thai red or green curry paste

½ stalk lemongrass, coarsely chopped

2 kaffir lime leaves, shredded

1 cup coconut milk

4 canned baby corn, halved

4 green beans, cut into ¾-inch pieces

¼ pound frozen or fresh, peeled cooked shrimp

6 tablespoons cooked microwave jasmine rice

**TO SERVE**

Chopped fresh cilantro

*This aromatic curry is cooked in coconut milk that has been infused with lemongrass and kaffir lime leaves. Choose between red or green curry paste—green is usually slightly hotter.*

**1** In a large mug, stir together the curry paste, lemongrass, kaffir lime leaves, and coconut milk. Microwave on high for 2 minutes.

**2** Stir in the baby corn and green beans and cook on high for 2 to 3 minutes, or until just tender.

**3** Add the shrimp, stir well, and cook on high for 2 minutes if frozen or 1 minute if fresh.

**4** Add the rice and cook on high for 1 minute. Stir well and serve immediately with cilantro sprinkled on top.

# PANCETTA AND DOLCELATTE RISOTTO

**SERVES 1**

*Prep / cook time: 11 minutes*

*Microwave: 1000W
(see page 5)*

1 teaspoon olive oil

2 tablespoons diced pancetta

1 tablespoon chopped onion

1 teaspoon garlic paste

¼ cup Arborio rice

1⅔ cups hot chicken stock

2 tablespoons chopped dolcelatte cheese or other creamy blue cheese

Large handful of baby spinach

Freshly ground black pepper

*This simple supper dish is full of flavor. You could add any creamy blue cheese, such as Gorgonzola, but don't be tempted to add more salt, as the pancetta and cheese are already quite salty.*

**1** Put the oil, pancetta, onion, and garlic paste in a large mug and microwave on high for 1 minute.

**2** Stir in the rice and pour in ½ cup of the stock. Stand the mug in a shallow microwaveable bowl, just in case any liquid boils over. Microwave on high for 2 minutes. Stir, then pour in another ½ cup of the stock and cook on high for 2 minutes. Repeat until all the stock has been used up and the rice is just tender.

**3** Stir in the dolcelatte and spinach and allow to stand for 1 minute, until the spinach has wilted. Season to taste with pepper and serve immediately.

SERVES 1

# WILD MUSHROOM RISOTTO

Prep / cook time: 15 minutes,
plus 10 minutes soaking time
for the mushrooms

Microwave: 1000W
(see page 5)

2 tablespoons dried wild
mushrooms

1⅔ cups hot chicken
or vegetable stock

¼ cup Arborio rice

1 to 2 tablespoons freshly grated
Parmesan cheese

1 tablespoon chopped fresh
flat-leaf parsley

Salt and freshly ground
black pepper

Truffle oil, to drizzle (optional)

*Dried mushrooms are a great pantry standby and
are packed full of flavor. This risotto uses only a few
ingredients, but it tastes delicious.*

**1** Put the mushrooms in a large mug. Add ½ cup of the
stock. Allow to soak for 10 minutes.

**2** Stir in the rice. Stand the mug in a shallow
microwaveable bowl, just in case any liquid boils over.
Microwave on high for 2 minutes. Stir, then pour
over ¼ cup of the stock and microwave for 1 minute.
Repeat until all the stock has been used up and the
rice is just tender.

**3** Stir in the Parmesan and parsley and allow to stand
for 1 minute. Season to taste with salt and pepper and
serve immediately with a drizzle of truffle oil (if using).

# SPAGHETTI CARBONARA

SERVES 1

*Prep / cook time: 9 to 10 minutes*

*Microwave: 1000W*
*(see page 5)*

2 slices smoked bacon, chopped

1 garlic clove (crushed in a garlic press or smashed with a knife)

22 strands spaghetti, broken into pieces

⅔ cup boiling water

4 tablespoons light cream cheese

2 tablespoons milk

2 tablespoons freshly grated Parmesan cheese

1 tablespoon chopped fresh parsley

Freshly ground black pepper

*A classic Italian favorite, this dish is traditionally cooked using eggs and cream. However, this recipe is slightly healthier because it uses reduced-fat cream cheese instead.*

**1** Put the bacon and garlic in a large mug and microwave on high for 1 minute. Remove and stir to break up the bacon.

**2** Add the spaghetti and water and microwave on high for 1 minute, then stir well. Return to the microwave and cook on medium for 2 minutes more.

**3** Stir in the cream cheese and milk and microwave on high for 2 minutes. Stir and microwave for 2 minutes more, or until the pasta is just cooked.

**4** Stir in the Parmesan and parsley. Allow to stand for 1 minute. Season to taste with pepper and serve.

**SERVES 1**

# MACARONI AND CHEESE

*Prep / cook time: 14 minutes*

*Microwave: 1000W
(see page 5)*

¼ cup macaroni

1¼ cups cold water

2 tablespoons cream cheese at room temperature

¼ teaspoon English mustard

2 tablespoons grated sharp Cheddar cheese

Salt and freshly ground black pepper

Truffle oil, to drizzle (optional)

*Presenting the ultimate comfort food: pasta coated in a tangy cheese sauce. You can make this even more delectable by drizzling it with a little truffle oil.*

**1** Put the macaroni in a large mug. Add 6 tablespoons of the water. Put the mug in a shallow microwaveable bowl (some of the water will boil over). Cover with plastic wrap and pierce with a knife. Microwave on high for 2 minutes.

**2** Stir well, pour any of the water in the bowl back into the mug, then add another ¼ cup of the water and microwave for 2 minutes more. Repeat the process 2 more times, or until the pasta is just tender, about 8 minutes in total.

**3** Stir in the remaining 2 tablespoons water, the cream cheese, mustard, and Cheddar. Return to the microwave and cook on high for 2 minutes.

**4** Stir well, then season to taste with salt and pepper and allow to stand for 1 minute. Serve with a little truffle oil (if using).

***To make macaroni with mustard, ham, and spinach:***
Cook macaroni as above, then stir in the 2 tablespoons water, cream cheese, 1 teaspoon whole-grain mustard, a handful of baby spinach leaves, and 1 slice ham, chopped. Cook for 2 minutes more. Season to taste with salt and pepper and allow to stand for 1 minute before serving.

# TOMATO PASTA WITH ZUCCHINI

**SERVES 1**

Prep / cook time: 6 minutes

Microwave: 1000W
(see page 5)

1 garlic clove (crushed in a garlic press or smashed with a knife)

½ small zucchini, diced

40 pieces fresh fusilli pasta (4.5 ounces)

¼ cup plus 3 tablespoons (7 tablespoons) boiling water

¼ cup tomato sauce

2 tablespoons mascarpone cheese

2 basil leaves, shredded

#### TO SERVE

Freshly ground black pepper

Green salad

Crusty bread

*Fresh pasta cooks really quickly in the microwave. Some penne pasta would work well here, too, if you want something other than fusilli.*

**1** Put the garlic, zucchini, and pasta in a large mug. Pour in the boiling water and stir. Cover with plastic wrap and pierce with a knife.

**2** Stand the mug in a shallow microwaveable bowl, as some of the water may boil over. Microwave on high for 2 minutes. Remove and stir well, then stir in the tomato sauce and mascarpone, cover again with the plastic wrap, and microwave on medium for 2 minutes, or until the pasta is just cooked.

**3** Stir in the basil and allow to stand for 1 minute before serving with freshly ground black pepper, a crisp green salad, and crusty bread.

# SPAGHETTI BOLOGNESE

SERVES 1

*Prep / cook time: 10 minutes*

*Microwave: 1000W (see page 5)*

½ teaspoon olive oil

2 tablespoons chopped onion

3 tablespoons ground beef

4 mushrooms, chopped

1½ cups canned chopped tomatoes

½ teaspoon Italian seasoning

8 strands spaghetti, broken into pieces

Salt and freshly ground black pepper

### TO SERVE

1 tablespoon freshly grated Parmesan cheese

*This Italian classic is ridiculously easy to prepare in a mug using only a few ingredients.*

**1** Place the oil, onion, and beef in a large mug. Stir well, then microwave on high for 1 minute.

**2** Remove and break up the beef with a fork. Stir in the mushrooms, tomatoes, Italian seasoning, spaghetti, and salt and pepper to taste.

**3** Stand the mug in a shallow microwaveable bowl, in case any of the mixture boils over. Microwave on high for 2 minutes. Remove, stir well, and microwave on high for 2 minutes more.

**4** Stir again and cook for 2 minutes more, or until the spaghetti is cooked. Allow to stand for 1 minute before serving with the Parmesan.

# CHILI CON CARNE

*Prep / cook time: 6 minutes*

*Microwave: 1000W
(see page 5)*

1 teaspoon sunflower oil

2 tablespoons chopped onion

¼ cup ground beef

1 teaspoon chili powder, or to taste

½ teaspoon unsweetened cocoa powder

¼ cup canned chopped tomatoes

1½ cups canned red kidney beans, drained and rinsed

Salt and freshly ground black pepper

6 tablespoons cooked microwave long-grain rice

## TO SERVE

Sour cream

Cornbread (see page 58)

*This well-known spicy dish is sure to become a midweek favorite. Try it served with the homemade cornbread on page 58.*

**1** Put the oil, onion, and beef in a large mug. Microwave on high for 1 minute, then stir with a fork to break up the beef.

**2** Add the chili powder, cocoa powder, tomatoes, and kidney beans and microwave on high for 2 minutes.

**3** Season to taste with salt and pepper and stir well, then put the rice on top. Cover with plastic wrap and pierce with a knife. Microwave on high for 1 minute. Stir the rice into the chili mixture and allow to stand for 1 minute.

**4** Serve with a dollop of sour cream and a slice of cornbread.

# SPINACH AND RICOTTA LASAGNA

SERVES
2

*Prep / cook time: 10 minutes*

*Microwave: 1000W*
*(see page 5)*

**Eight 2-inch chunks of frozen spinach**

**2 large fresh lasagna sheets**

**¼ cup ricotta cheese**

**1 tablespoon pine nuts (optional)**

**½ teaspoon ground nutmeg**

**Salt and freshly ground black pepper**

**2 tablespoons tomato sauce**

**4 tablespoons shredded mozzarella**

**1 tablespoon freshly grated Parmesan cheese**

**TO SERVE**

**Green salad**

*Lasagna for two is so simple to make. Use coffee cups; they're wider than mugs and allow for more even cooking.*

**1** Put the spinach in a microwaveable cup. Cover with plastic wrap and pierce with a knife. Microwave on high for 3 minutes.

**2** Cut each lasagna sheet into 6 pieces to fit the cups and place in a shallow bowl. Pour over enough boiling water to cover and leave for 30 seconds to 1 minute, until softened. Drain.

**3** Mix the spinach with the ricotta, pine nuts (if using), nutmeg, and salt and pepper to taste. Put 1 tablespoon of the tomato sauce in each of 2 medium microwaveable coffee cups.

**4** Add 2 pieces of lasagna to each cup. Don't worry if they go up the sides of the cup.

**5** Divide half the spinach mixture between the cups. Add 1 tablespoon of the mozzarella to each, then add another 2 pieces of lasagna and the remaining spinach mixture. Top with the remaining lasagna pieces, then spoon over the remaining mozzarella, spreading it to cover the lasagna.

**6** Sprinkle with the Parmesan. Microwave on high for 4 minutes, until bubbling.

**7** Allow to stand for 2 minutes before serving with a crisp green salad.

# JAMBALAYA WITH SHRIMP AND CHORIZO

**SERVES 1**

*Prep / cook time: 15 minutes*

*Microwave: 1000W
(see page 5)*

2 tablespoons chopped fresh chorizo sausage

1 tablespoon chopped onion

¼ cup long-grain rice

1¼ cups plus 2 tablespoons hot chicken stock

¼ cup canned chopped tomatoes

1 teaspoon Italian seasoning

¼ each small red and green bell peppers, seeded and diced

2 tablespoons frozen peas

6 cooked and peeled jumbo shrimp

1 scallion, chopped

Dash of Tabasco sauce (optional)

*This lightly spiced Cajun rice dish comes from Louisiana. If you prefer, replace the shrimp with some diced chicken breast; just add it to the mug when you stir in the rice.*

**1** Put the chorizo and onion in a large mug. Microwave on high for 1 minute, until the paprika oil is released from the sausage.

**2** Stir in the rice until coated with the oil. Add ½ cup of the stock and microwave on high for 2 minutes. Stir in another ¼ cup of stock and microwave on high for 2 minutes.

**3** Stir in the tomatoes and Italian seasoning. Stand the mug in a shallow microwaveable bowl, to catch spills. Microwave on high for 3 minutes.

**4** Stir in ¼ cup of the stock and microwave on low for 3 minutes.

**5** Stir in another ¼ cup of stock and the bell peppers and microwave on low for 2 minutes.

**6** Stir in the peas, shrimp, and scallion (reserve a little scallion for garnish) and microwave on high for 2 minutes, or until the rice is tender and most of the liquid has been absorbed. Add a dash of Tabasco (if using) and serve garnished with the reserved scallion.

# CHICKEN STEW WITH HERBED DUMPLINGS

**SERVES 1**

Prep / cook time: 11 minutes

Microwave: 1000W
(see page 5)

2 tablespoons chopped onion

1 small carrot, peeled and chopped into ½-inch pieces

1 small potato, peeled and chopped into ½-inch pieces (2 to 3 tablespoons)

1 cup hot chicken stock

2 teaspoons granulated chicken bouillon

Handful of shredded cooked chicken (about 2 ounces)

Pinch of dried mixed herbs or 2 teaspoons chopped fresh parsley

### FOR THE DUMPLINGS

2 tablespoons self-rising flour

1 tablespoon butter

½ teaspoon dried oregano

4 teaspoons water

*A comforting main all in one mug. Follow this up with a Sticky Toffee Pudding (see page 106) for a British meal.*

**1** Put the vegetables in a large mug. Add ½ cup of the stock and stand the mug in a shallow microwaveable dish. Cover the mug with plastic wrap and pierce with a knife. Microwave on high for 2 minutes.

**2** Stir, then cover, return to the microwave, and cook on high for 2 minutes.

**3** Meanwhile, make the dumplings. In a small cup, mix the flour, butter, oregano, and water. Stir the remaining stock, bouillon granules, chicken, and herbs into the vegetables in the mug.

**4** Using a spoon, divide the dumpling mixture in half and dollop both on top of the stew. Cover again with the plastic wrap and microwave on high for 1 minute to 1 minute 30 seconds, or until the dumplings are just set.

**5** Allow to stand for 2 to 3 minutes before serving.

# SWEET POTATO AND CHICKPEA TAGINE

**SERVES 1**

*Prep / cook time: 10 minutes*

*Microwave: 1000W
(see page 5)*

1 teaspoon vegetable oil

1 tablespoon chopped onion

½ teaspoon garlic paste

1 teaspoon ras el hanout
(Moroccan spice blend)

¼ sweet potato (about 3 ounces),
peeled and chopped into ¾-inch
pieces

¼ cup plus 3 tablespoons
(7 tablespoons) vegetable stock
or water

¼ cup canned chopped tomatoes

4 dried apricots, chopped

3 tablespoons canned chickpeas

½ teaspoon harissa paste

2 green olives, sliced

### TO GARNISH

4 almonds

½ preserved lemon (optional), pith
removed and peel cut into thin strips

### TO SERVE

Fruity Couscous (page 59)

*This healthy vegetarian Moroccan stew is packed
full of flavor. Serve with plain couscous or Fruity
Couscous (see page 59). The preserved lemon adds a
lovely citrus flavor; preserved lemons are available in
the international section of many supermarkets.*

**1** Put the oil, onion, garlic paste, and ras el hanout in a
large mug and microwave on high for 1 minute. Stir in
the sweet potato and ¼ cup of the stock. Cover with
plastic wrap and pierce with a knife.

**2** Microwave on high for 2 minutes. Stir well, then
microwave on high for 2 minutes more, or until the sweet
potato is just tender.

**3** Stir in the tomatoes, apricots, chickpeas, and the
remaining stock. Microwave on medium for 3 minutes.

**4** Stir in the harissa paste and olives and allow to stand
for 1 minute. Garnish with the almonds and preserved
lemon (if using) and serve with Fruity Couscous.

# SALMON WITH PARSLEY AND MASHED POTATOES

SERVES 1

*Prep / cook time: 7 to 9 minutes*

*Microwave: 1000W*
*(see page 5)*

1 tablespoon butter

2 tablespoons all-purpose flour

⅔ cup milk

1 tablespoon crème fraîche
or heavy cream (optional)

2 tablespoons chopped fresh
parsley

Salt and freshly ground
black pepper

1 small skinless salmon fillet,
cubed (5 to 6 ounces)

2 tablespoons frozen peas

6 heaping tablespoons chilled
mashed potato

*Substitute your favorite fish for the salmon—cod or smoked haddock would work well—or add some cooked peeled shrimp.*

**1** Put the butter, flour, and milk in a large mug. Microwave on high for 30 seconds, then whisk.

**2** Return the mug to the microwave and cook for 30 seconds more, then whisk again. Repeat until the sauce thickens. Don't be tempted to ignore the 30-second intervals or the sauce may go lumpy!

**3** Stir in the crème fraîche (if using) and parsley and season to taste with salt and pepper. Add the fish and peas, then top with the mashed potato and sprinkle with the cheese (if using).

**4** Stand the mug in a microwaveable bowl, as some of the sauce may boil over. Microwave on low for 3 to 4 minutes, or until the fish is cooked. Allow to stand for 2 minutes before serving.

# SPICY LAMB MEATBALLS

SERVES 1

*Prep/cook time: 9 minutes*

*Microwave: 1000W
(see page 5)*

¼ cup ground lamb

½ teaspoon ground cumin

½ teaspoon ground coriander

2 teaspoons chopped fresh
cilantro, plus extra to garnish

Salt and freshly ground
black pepper

5 tablespoons canned chopped
tomatoes with chiles

¼ red bell pepper, seeded and cut
into thin strips

**TO SERVE**

A little chopped fresh cilantro

Flatbreads and/or couscous

*These Middle Eastern–inspired meatballs are
ridiculously easy to prepare and cook. They're also
delicious served with Fruity Couscous (see page 59),
or flatbreads and maybe a spoonful of yogurt.*

**1** Mix the lamb, cumin, coriander, and cilantro and
season well with salt and pepper. Using your hands, mix
the ingredients together, then roll between your palms to
make 6 small meatballs.

**2** Place the meatballs in a medium mug. Cover with
plastic wrap and pierce with a knife.

**3** Microwave on high for 1 minute. Stir in the tomatoes
and bell pepper, cover again, and microwave on medium
for 3 minutes. Stir, cover again, return to the microwave,
and cook on medium for 1 minute.

**4** Allow to stand for 1 minute, then garnish with a little
cilantro. Serve with flatbread and couscous, if desired.

# SWEET-AND-SOUR CHICKEN

**SERVES 2**

*Prep / cook time: 10 minutes*

*Microwave: 1000W*
*(see page 5)*

## FOR THE SAUCE

**One 8-ounce can juice-packed pineapple chunks**

**2 tablespoons ketchup**

**1 tablespoon light brown sugar**

**1 tablespoon dark soy sauce**

**1 tablespoon white wine vinegar**

**1 teaspoon ginger paste**

**1 teaspoon garlic paste**

## FOR THE REST

**4 teaspoons cornstarch**

**1 large boneless, skinless chicken breast, cut into small cubes**

**½ red bell pepper, seeded and cut into chunks**

**2 scallions, chopped**

**5 to 6 ounces instant ramen noodles**

*Cook this Chinese favorite in less time than it takes to order from your local take-out joint! There are quite a lot of ingredients, but don't let that put you off: most are pantry staples.*

**1** Make the sauce. Drain the juice from the pineapple into a 2-cup measuring cup. Measure out and set aside 2 tablespoons of juice and ¼ cup of the pineapple. Stir the ketchup, brown sugar, soy sauce, vinegar, and pastes into the measuring cup. Add cold water to make 9 fluid ounces.

**2** Add 2 teaspoons of the cornstarch and 1 tablespoon of the reserved pineapple juice to each of 2 large mugs and stir well. Divide the chicken, bell pepper, and scallions between the mugs and mix well.

**3** Divide the sauce between the 2 mugs, stir well, and microwave on high for 2 minutes. Stir in the reserved pineapple pieces. Cover with plastic wrap and pierce with a knife.

**4** Return the mugs to the microwave and cook on low for 4 minutes. Stir well. Break the noodles in half, add half to each mug, cover, and microwave on low for 2 minutes.

**5** Stir well and allow to stand for 1 minute before serving.

**SERVES 1**

# BEEF COBBLER

*Prep / cook time: 8 minutes*

*Microwave: 1000W
(see page 5)*

1 teaspoon vegetable oil

1 tablespoon chopped onion

¼ cup ground beef

½ carrot, peeled and chopped

2 small red potatoes, quartered

½ cup store-bought beef gravy

2 tablespoons frozen peas

**FOR THE TOPPING**

2 tablespoons butter, softened

¼ cup self-rising flour

2 tablespoons milk

*This hearty meal makes a perfect Sunday lunch.
Use a cup rather than a mug to make it; otherwise
the cobbler will sink.*

**1** Put the oil, onion, and beef in a medium cup. Microwave on high for 1 minute, then stir with a fork to break up the beef.

**2** Add the carrot, potatoes, and gravy to the beef, stir well, and stand the cup in a shallow microwaveable bowl, as some of the liquid will boil over. Cover with plastic wrap and pierce with a knife.

**3** Microwave on medium for 2 minutes. Add the peas, stir well, cover again with the plastic wrap, then return to the microwave and cook on medium for 1 minute, or until the vegetables are just tender.

**4** Meanwhile, make the topping. In a small cup or bowl, rub the butter into the flour, then mix with the milk to form a slightly sticky dough.

**5** Divide the dough into two pieces, roll into balls, and flatten slightly. Arrange over the top of the beef, cover the cup with plastic wrap and pierce with a knife, then return to the microwave and cook on medium for 2 minutes.

**6** Allow to stand for 2 minutes before serving.

# SWEETS
### AND
# BAKING

# CHOCOLATE AND PISTACHIO BROWNIE

**SERVES 1**

*Prep / cook time: 1 minute*

*Microwave: 1000W*
*(see page 5)*

2 tablespoons all-purpose flour

2 tablespoons light brown sugar

1 tablespoon unsweetened cocoa powder

Pinch of salt

1 tablespoon sunflower oil

2 tablespoons milk

1 tablespoon chopped pistachios

1 tablespoon dark or milk chocolate chips

*This delicious brownie (pictured on page 92) is slightly gooey on the inside. You can substitute any chopped nuts, such as macadamias, for the pistachios if you prefer. Serve warm with a scoop of ice cream.*

**1** In a medium mug or cup, mix the flour, brown sugar, cocoa powder, and salt, then stir in the oil and milk until you have a smooth batter with no lumps. Stir in the pistachios and chocolate chips.

**2** Microwave on high for 1 minute.

# WHITE CHOCOLATE LIME CHEESECAKES

**SERVES 2**

*Prep / cook time: 4 minutes,*
*plus 30 minutes chilling time*

*Microwave: 1000W*
*(see page 5)*

**2 tablespoons butter, softened**

**4 graham crackers, crushed**

**1 tablespoon dark chocolate chips**

**⅓ cup good-quality white chocolate, broken into small pieces**

**Finely grated zest of 1 small lime**

**1 cup mascarpone cheese**

**1 tablespoon powdered sugar, sifted**

### TO DECORATE

**Grated lime zest**

**Grated white chocolate**

*This no-cook cheesecake is a breeze to make. The creamy, tangy filling is complemented by a chocolatey graham cracker base.*

**1** Put 1 tablespoon of the butter in each of 2 medium microwaveable teacups. Microwave on high for 30 seconds to 1 minute, or until the butter has melted. Mix the crushed graham crackers with the dark chocolate chips and divide the mixture between the cups. Mix with the melted butter, then press down with the back of a spoon. Place in the fridge to set while you make the filling.

**2** In a small microwaveable bowl, melt the white chocolate on medium for 1 minute, stir, then microwave in 30-second intervals until melted. Stir well, then beat in the lime zest, mascarpone, and powdered sugar.

**3** Spoon the mixture over the graham cracker base and chill in the refrigerator for 30 minutes, or until set. Decorate with a little lime zest and white chocolate.

 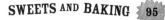

# LEMON CAKE

SERVES 1

*Prep / cook time: 3 minutes, plus 4 minutes standing time*

*Microwave: 1000W (see page 5)*

**FOR THE SPONGE**

**1 tablespoon butter, softened**

**3 tablespoons granulated sugar**

**Finely grated zest of 1 lemon**

**3 tablespoons milk**

**3 tablespoons self-rising flour**

**½ beaten egg**

**FOR THE SAUCE**

**2 tablespoons boiling water**

**1 teaspoon butter, softened**

**2 tablespoons light brown sugar**

**Juice of 1 lemon**

*This cake separates into two layers, a light sponge and a tangy sauce, as it cooks in minutes.*

**1** Make the sponge. Put the butter in a large mug. Microwave on high for 30 seconds to melt. Stir in the granulated sugar, lemon zest, milk, flour, and egg and beat until smooth.

**2** Make the sauce. Pour the boiling water into a small bowl. Add the butter, stir until melted, then stir in the brown sugar and lemon juice. Carefully pour the sauce over the sponge mixture, then microwave on high for 2 minutes, or until just cooked in the center.

**3** Allow to stand for 4 minutes before serving, as the sauce will be extremely hot.

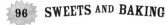

# AFFOGATO AL CAFFÈ

SERVES 2

Prep time: 2 minutes

**4 scoops good-quality
vanilla ice cream**

**2 freshly brewed espressos (made
with espresso powder or with an
espresso machine, if you're feeling
fancy)**

**TO SERVE**

**2 amaretti cookies**

*Hot coffee over cold ice cream! This must be
the simplest dessert in the world to make.*

**1** Scoop 2 balls of the ice cream into each of 2 cappuccino
cups or latte glasses. Pour a cup of hot espresso quickly
over each.

**2** Serve immediately, with the cookies on the side
for dunking.

# RASPBERRY AND LEMON GELATIN

SERVES
2

Prep / cook time: 3 minutes, plus
40 minutes chilling time.

Microwave: 1000W
(see page 5)

**3 tablespoons raspberry Jell-O powder**

**½ cup boiling water**

**1 cup lemonade, chilled**

**14 frozen raspberries**

*Serve these pretty gelatins in glass cups or small glass latte mugs. You can easily double the recipe to make four—perfect for entertaining! Using frozen raspberries makes the gelatin set more quickly.*

**1** Put the Jell-O powder in a microwaveable measuring cup, add the boiling water, and stir until the gelatin has dissolved. If the gelatin does not dissolve thoroughly, microwave on high for 30 seconds.

**2** Once all the gelatin has dissolved, stir in the lemonade and raspberries. Divide between two 7-ounce glass mugs or cups and refrigerate for about 40 minutes, or until set.

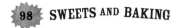

# BERRY CRUMBLE

**SERVES 1**

*Prep / cook time: 3 minutes*

*Microwave: 1000W*
*(see page 5)*

**½ cup mixed frozen berries (raspberries, blueberries, or blackberries)**

**1 teaspoon light brown sugar**

**1 teaspoon cornstarch**

**FOR THE TOPPING**

**¼ cup rolled oats**

**2 teaspoons light brown sugar**

**¼ teaspoon ground cinnamon**

**1 teaspoon butter, melted**

**TO SERVE**

**Vanilla ice cream or heavy cream**

*A really simple, delicious crumble that you can adapt with any of your favorite frozen berries.*

**1** Put the berries in a small mug; they should almost come up to the top. Sprinkle the brown sugar and cornstarch over them and microwave on high for 30 seconds. Stir gently so you don't break up the berries, then microwave on high for 30 seconds, or until the sauce starts to thicken.

**2** Make the topping. Put the oats in a small cup or bowl and stir in the brown sugar, cinnamon, and melted butter. Spoon the topping over the berries and stand the cup in a microwaveable shallow bowl, in case any of the sauce bubbles over. Microwave on high for 1 minute 20 seconds.

**3** Allow to stand for 1 minute before serving with a scoop of vanilla ice cream or a splash of heavy cream.

# TOFFEE AND BANANA SPONGE CAKE

**SERVES 2**

*Prep / cook time: 5 minutes*

*Microwave: 1000W*
*(see page 5)*

**FOR THE TOFFEE SAUCE**

2 tablespoons butter

4 tablespoons light brown sugar

2 tablespoons evaporated or whole milk

**FOR THE SPONGE CAKE**

1 ripe banana

3 tablespoons all-purpose flour

¼ teaspoon baking powder

¼ teaspoon baking soda

2 tablespoons light brown sugar

½ teaspoon vanilla extract

1 egg, beaten

1 tablespoon milk

1 tablespoon sunflower oil

10 pecans, broken into pieces

*Banana and toffee make a perfect combination, and this recipe is also a great way to use overripe bananas. It's delicious served with cream.*

**1** Make the toffee sauce. Put the butter, brown sugar, and milk in a small microwaveable cup or bowl and microwave on high for 30 seconds. Stir, then microwave for 30 seconds more.

**2** Make the sponge cake. Put the banana in a small bowl and mash it with a fork. Stir in the flour, baking powder, baking soda, brown sugar, vanilla, egg, milk, oil, and pecans.

**3** Divide half the toffee sauce between 2 medium mugs, then divide the banana mixture between the mugs.

**4** Microwave on high for 2 minutes 30 seconds. Allow to stand for 1 minute, then pour the remaining toffee sauce over the top and serve.

# MELTING CHOCOLATE CAKES

**SERVES 2**

*Prep/cook time: 3 minutes*

*Microwave: 1000W*
*(see page 5)*

**¼ cup dark chocolate chips**

**2 tablespoons butter, softened**

**2 tablespoons sugar**

**½ teaspoon vanilla extract**

**1 tablespoon all-purpose flour**

**1 egg, beaten**

*These chocolatey cakes have a gooey center. They're delicious served with a scoop of vanilla or pistachio ice cream—a good bake for date night.*

**1** Put the chocolate chips and butter in a small microwaveable bowl or large mug and microwave on high for 1 minute. Remove and stir, then return to the microwave and cook on high for 20 to 30 seconds, or until the butter and chocolate are completely melted. Stir well.

**2** Stir in the sugar, vanilla, flour, and egg and keep stirring until all the ingredients are combined.

**3** Divide the mixture equally between 2 small mugs or cups and microwave on high for 40 to 50 seconds.

**4** Allow to stand for 1 minute before serving.

# STICKY GINGERBREAD

SERVES 2

Prep / cook time: 5 minutes,
plus cooling

Microwave: 1000W
(see page 5)

2 tablespoons softened butter,
plus extra for greasing

¼ cup molasses

¼ cup dark brown sugar

2 tablespoons milk

¼ teaspoon baking soda

1 piece of preserved ginger,
from a jar, chopped, plus
2 tablespoons of the ginger syrup

1 teaspoon ground ginger

½ teaspoon ground cinnamon

½ cup all-purpose flour

1 egg, beaten

*This recipe is cozy for the holidays. If you have time,
make it the day before and wrap it in foil to keep it
moist.*

**1** Lightly butter 2 medium mugs and line the bottoms
with parchment paper.

**2** Put the 2 tablespoons butter, molasses, and brown
sugar in a microwaveable measuring cup and microwave
on high for 2 minutes, until the mixture is boiling.

**3** Add the milk and baking soda, then stir in the
preserved ginger, ground ginger, cinnamon, flour, and
egg. Mix well, then divide the batter between the 2 mugs.

**4** Microwave on high for 2 minutes; the mixture may look
slightly wet in the middle. Allow to stand for 1 minute.

**5** Cool slightly, then run a knife blade around the edge of
each cup. Drizzle the ginger syrup over each gingerbread
and allow to cool.

**6** Remove from the mug and allow to cool completely.

# STICKY TOFFEE PUDDING

SERVES 1

*Cook/prep time: 6 minutes, plus cooling*

*Microwave: 1000W (see page 5)*

**FOR THE PUDDING**

**5 pitted dates, coarsely chopped**

**1 tablespoon boiling water**

**¼ teaspoon baking soda**

**1 tablespoon butter, softened**

**1 tablespoon light brown sugar**

**1 tablespoon self-rising flour**

**½ beaten egg**

**FOR THE TOFFEE SAUCE**

**1 tablespoon light brown sugar**

**1 tablespoon butter, softened**

**1 tablespoon crème fraîche**

**TO SERVE**

**Vanilla ice cream**

*A rich and indulgent classic British dessert, drizzled with a simple toffee sauce . . . although you may need a brisk walk afterward!*

**1** Make the pudding. Put the dates in a medium mug. Add the boiling water and microwave on high for 30 seconds. Remove and stir in the baking soda; the mixture will fizz. Allow to stand for 30 seconds, then stir to break up the dates.

**2** Add the butter to the dates and microwave on high for 10 to 20 seconds, or until melted. Stir in the sugar, flour, and egg and mix well. Microwave on high for 1 minute 30 seconds, until risen and spongy. Allow to stand for 1 minute.

**3** Make the toffee sauce. Put the sugar, butter, and crème fraîche in a small microwaveable cup or bowl and microwave on high for 30 seconds. Stir well, then microwave on high for another 30 seconds. Pour over the top of the pudding, pulling away the sides of the sponge so that the sauce can soak through.

**4** Serve immediately with vanilla ice cream.

# STRAWBERRY BAKED CHEESECAKES

**SERVES 2**

*Prep / cook time: 6 minutes,
plus 2 hours chilling time*

*Microwave: 1000W
(see page 5)*

2 tablespoons butter

4 graham crackers, crushed

**FOR THE FILLING**

8 ounces cream cheese

¼ cup crème fraîche or
sour cream

1 teaspoon vanilla extract

1 teaspoon finely grated lemon zest

¼ cup sugar

1 egg, beaten

**TO DECORATE**

Sliced strawberries

Strawberry sauce

*New York–style cheesecake is traditionally baked
slowly in the oven; however, this method produces a
similar result, with only a small amount of effort and
time. Try it topped with blueberries if you prefer.*

**1** Put 1 tablespoon of the butter in each of 2 medium
cups; glass ones are ideal. Microwave on high for
30 seconds to 1 minute, or until the butter has melted.

**2** Divide the graham cracker crumbs between the 2 cups,
stir well until combined, then press down with the back
of a spoon. Microwave on medium for 1 minute
30 seconds, or until the crumbs start to puff up. Put the
cups in the fridge to chill while you make the filling.

**3** Make the filling. In a small bowl, beat the cream
cheese, crème fraîche, vanilla, lemon zest, sugar, and egg.
Divide the filling between the cups, then microwave on
medium for 2 minutes 30 seconds to 3 minutes, or until
the outsides are firm but the centers are slightly wobbly.

**4** Allow to cool slightly, then refrigerate for 2 hours.
Decorate with fresh strawberries and a drizzle of
strawberry sauce to serve.

# COFFEE AND WALNUT CAKE

**SERVES 1**

*Prep / cook time: 3 minutes*

*Microwave: 1000W
(see page 5)*

### FOR THE CAKE

**2 tablespoons softened butter, plus extra for greasing**

**1 tablespoon coffee syrup**

**2 tablespoons self-rising flour**

**2 tablespoons light brown sugar**

**1 tablespoon chopped walnuts**

**½ beaten egg**

### FOR THE ICING

**2 tablespoons mascarpone cheese**

**1 tablespoon powdered sugar**

**½ teaspoon coffee syrup**

### TO DECORATE

**2 walnut halves**

*This moist cake is topped with a delicious coffee-flavored icing and is so quick and easy to make. Whip this cake up for afternoon tea or stick a candle in it for a speedy birthday treat!*

**1** Make the cake. Lightly butter a medium mug. Add the 2 tablespoons butter and microwave on high for 30 seconds to 1 minute, or until melted. Stir in the coffee syrup, flour, brown sugar, walnuts, and egg and mix well.

**2** Microwave on high for 1 minute, until risen and spongy. Allow to stand for 1 minute, then if you prefer, remove from the cup and allow to cool.

**3** Make the icing. Beat the mascarpone with the powdered sugar and coffee syrup until smooth.

**4** Spread the top of the cake with the icing and decorate with the walnut halves.

# HONEY PUDDING

**SERVES 1**

*Cook / prep time: 5 minutes*

*Microwave: 1000W*
*(see page 5)*

**2 tablespoons softened butter plus extra for greasing**

**2 tablespoons honey**

**½ teaspoon fresh lemon juice**

**2 tablespoons sugar**

**½ beaten egg**

**2 tablespoons self-rising flour**

**1 teaspoon milk**

**TO SERVE**

**Ice cream**

*You can easily double the ingredients in this recipe and put it in two mugs to serve two; simply cook it for two more minutes. This is delicious served with ice cream.*

**1** Lightly butter a medium mug. Spoon 1 tablespoon of the honey over the bottom and add the lemon juice.

**2** In a small cup or bowl, cream together the 2 tablespoons butter and sugar, then beat in the egg. Stir in the flour and milk, then add it to the honey in the mug.

**3** Microwave on high for 2 minutes, until risen and spongy. Drizzle with the remaining honey and allow to stand for 1 minute before serving.

**4** Serve with ice cream.

# CREAMY VANILLA RICE PUDDING

SERVES 1

Prep / cook time: 15 minutes

Microwave: 1000W
(see page 5)

¼ cup Arborio rice

½ teaspoon vanilla extract

2 teaspoons sugar

1¼ cups boiling water

¼ cup plus 3 tablespoons
(7 tablespoons) evaporated milk

TO SERVE

Fruit preserves

Sliced almonds

*This recipe calls for risotto rice because it cooks quickly and has a nice creamy texture. If you'd like to treat yourself to chocolate rice pudding, at the end of the cooking time simply add four chunks of chopped milk or dark chocolate and stir until melted.*

**1** Put the rice in a large mug. Stir in the vanilla, sugar, and ½ cup of the boiling water. Stand the mug in a shallow microwaveable bowl, in case any of the liquid boils over. Microwave on high for 3 minutes.

**2** Stir the rice and add another ½ cup of the boiling water. Microwave on medium for 3 minutes more. Stir in the remaining boiling water and microwave on low for 3 minutes.

**3** Stir in half of the evaporated milk and microwave on low for 2 minutes. Stir in the remaining milk and microwave for 2 to 3 minutes, or until the rice is tender.

**4** Allow to stand for 2 minutes before serving with a dollop of fruit preserves and some almonds sprinkled over the top.

# CHOCOLATE ORANGE PUDDING

SERVES 1

*Prep / cook time: 4 minutes*

*Microwave: 1000W
(see page 5)*

**1 slice white bread, crusts removed**

**Softened butter, for spreading**

**6 chunks of dark chocolate, coarsely chopped (about 2 tablespoons)**

**1 egg**

**2 tablespoons sugar**

**Grated zest of 1 orange**

**¼ cup plus 3 tablespoons (7 tablespoons) milk**

*This gooey bread-and-butter pudding is so easy to make. You can vary it by using a flavored dark chocolate, such as ginger or chile, or you could try milk chocolate instead.*

**1** Spread the bread with butter, then cut it into squares. Arrange the squares in the bottom of a medium microwaveable coffee cup. Add the chocolate pieces, nestling them among the pieces of bread.

**2** In a small bowl or measuring cup, whisk the egg, sugar, orange zest, and milk until the sugar has dissolved. Pour this over the bread mixture.

**3** Microwave on high for about 1 minute 50 seconds, or until just set. Allow to stand for 1 minute before serving.

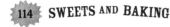

# CHRISTMAS PUDDING

**SERVES 2**

*Prep / cook time: 8 minutes*

*Microwave: 1000W*
*(see page 5)*

2 tablespoons softened butter
or margarine, plus extra for
greasing

2 tablespoons light brown sugar

1 egg

2 tablespoons all-purpose flour

1 teaspoon pumpkin pie spice

4 candied cherries, halved

½ cup mixed dried fruit

1 tablespoon molasses

5 tablespoons fresh bread crumbs

1 tablespoon brandy (optional)

*Making this fruity pudding in a cup will give it a nice round shape. When you remove it from the microwave, pour over a tablespoon of brandy for extra flavor. You can ignite it—just watch your eyebrows.*

**1** Lightly grease a medium microwaveable cup. Add the butter and brown sugar to the cup and cream together. Add the egg, flour, and pumpkin pie spice and stir until the mixture is smooth.

**2** Stir in the cherries, dried fruit, molasses, and bread crumbs until well combined.

**3** Cover the top loosely with plastic wrap and pierce with a knife. Microwave on medium for 3 minutes 30 seconds. Pour over the brandy (if using).

**4** Allow to stand for 3 minutes before turning out and serving.

# DRINKS

# ULTIMATE HOT CHOCOLATE

**SERVES 1**

*Prep / cook time: 3 minutes*

*Microwave: 1000W*
*(see page 5)*

**1 cup milk**

**1 ounce dark or milk chocolate, broken into small pieces**

**1 to 2 teaspoons sugar, to taste (optional)**

**FOR THE TOPPING**

**Whipped cream**

**Small handful of mini marshmallows**

**Grated chocolate**

*Got the winter blues? Take off the chill with this indulgent hot chocolate (pictured on page 118). It's also delicious made with flavored chocolate, such as orange, mint, or coffee.*

**1** Pour the milk into a medium mug. Microwave on high for 1 minute, then add the chocolate and stir well.

**2** Return to the microwave and cook on high for 30 seconds, or until all the chocolate has melted and the drink is hot. Stir well and add sugar to taste.

**3** Swirl whipped cream on the top and decorate with the marshmallows and grated chocolate.

# HOT-HOT CHOCOLATE

**SERVES 1**

*Prep / cook time: 2 minutes*

*Microwave: 1000W
(see page 5)*

**1 cup whole or reduced-fat milk**

**Finely grated zest of ½ lime**

**1 ounce dark chocolate flavored
with chile, broken into small pieces**

**Sugar (optional)**

*This fiery hot chocolate is made by simply using chocolate infused with chile. You could use dark chocolate mixed with a little ground chili powder instead. Either way, this is a quick winter warmer with a kick!*

**1** Pour the milk into a medium mug and add the lime zest. Microwave on high for 1 minute, then add the chocolate and stir well.

**2** Return to the microwave and cook on high for 30 seconds, or until all the chocolate has melted and the drink is hot. Stir well and add sugar to taste (if using).

**3** Allow to cool slightly, then enjoy.

# MULLED CIDER WITH GINGER

**SERVES 1**

*Prep / cook time: 3 minutes,
plus 5 minutes cooling time*

*Microwave: 1000W
(see page 5)*

**1 cup cider**

**1 star anise**

**¾-inch piece fresh ginger,
peeled and thinly sliced**

**½ small apple, cored
and thinly sliced**

**1 strip lemon zest**

**1 teaspoon light brown sugar**

*Fresh ginger gives a spicy, warming kick to this cider.
For a really festive wintry taste, add a small cinnamon
stick, too.*

**1** Put the cider, anise, ginger, apple, lemon zest, and
brown sugar in a tall mug. Microwave on high for
1 minute. Stir well, then microwave on high for
40 seconds.

**2** Allow to stand for 5 minutes for the flavors to infuse
and the drink to cool slightly.

# VANILLA LATTE

**SERVES 1**

*Prep / cook time: 2 minutes*

*Microwave: 1000W
(see page 5)*

**2 teaspoons instant espresso powder**

**4 teaspoons boiling water**

**1 cup milk**

**2 teaspoons vanilla extract**

**1 to 2 teaspoons vanilla sugar, or to taste**

*You can make this breakfast beverage with fat-free milk for a skinny latte—or if you fancy something more indulgent, top it off with a swirl of whipped cream and a little grated chocolate.*

**1** Dissolve the coffee in the boiling water in a medium mug. Stir in the milk, vanilla, and vanilla sugar.

**2** Microwave on high for 1 minute. Stir well, return to the microwave, and cook for 30 seconds.

**3** Allow to cool slightly.

# CHILL-OUT MILK

**SERVES 1**

*Prep / cook time: 2 minutes*

*Microwave: 1000W (see page 5)*

**1 cup milk**

**2 teaspoons honey**

**Pinch of ground cinnamon**

**Pinch of ground nutmeg**

*A bedtime drink, ideal for helping you to get that elusive perfect night's sleep. Sweet dreams . . .*

**1** Put the milk, honey, cinnamon, and nutmeg in a medium mug.

**2** Microwave on high for 1 minute. Stir well, return to the microwave, and cook for 30 seconds, or until hot.

# INDEX